Ord. 4.51

W9-BBM-402

MAY 1976
RECEIVED
OHIO DOMINICAN
COLLEGE LIBRARY
COLUMBUS, OHIO
43219

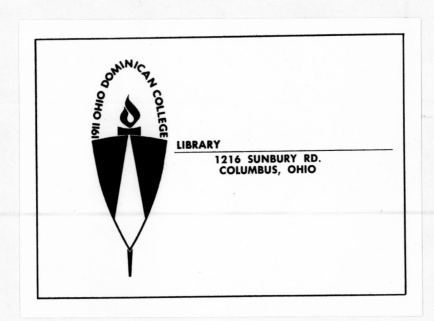

OHIO DOMINICAN COLLEGE 1911

LIBRARY

1216 SUNBURY RD.
COLUMBUS, OHIO

THE SUN

Newly Revised Edition

HERBERT S. ZIM

illustrated by Larry Kettelkamp
and photographs

William Morrow and Company
New York 1975

Copyright 1953, © 1975
by Herbert S. Zim
All rights reserved.
No part of this book may be reproduced
or utilized in any form or by any means,
electronic or mechanical,
including photocopying, recording
or by any information storage and
retrieval system, without permission
in writing from the Publisher.
Inquiries should be addressed to
William Morrow and Company, Inc.,
105 Madison Ave., New York, N.Y. 10016.
Printed in the United States of America.
1 2 3 4 5 79 78 77 76 75

Library of Congress
Cataloging in Publication Data

Zim, Herbert Spencer (date)
    The sun.
Summary: Discusses the sun's
heat, size, surface, and energy;
sunspots and their effects; and
the importance of the sun to the earth.
1. Sun—Juvenile literature.
[1. Sun] I. Kettelkamp, Larry, ill.
II. Title.
QB521.5.Z55 1975   523.7   74-34461
ISBN 0-688-22033-9
ISBN 0-688-32033-3 (lib. bdg.)

For advice and assistance
in this revision of *The Sun*,
the author wishes to thank
Dr. Joseph Davidson,
of the University of Miami,
and those who supplied
the excellent photographs,
a new feature of the book.

Metric measure,
now common the world over,
is used in this book.
Distances are in kilometers (km.);
weights, in grams (g.), kilograms (kg.),
or in metric tons of 1000 kg.;
and temperature in degrees Celsius (°C).
Compared with English measures:
1 kilometer = 0.6 miles
1 gram = 0.035 ounces
1 kilogram = 2.2 pounds
100° Celsius = 212° Fahrenheit

J.
523.7
Z

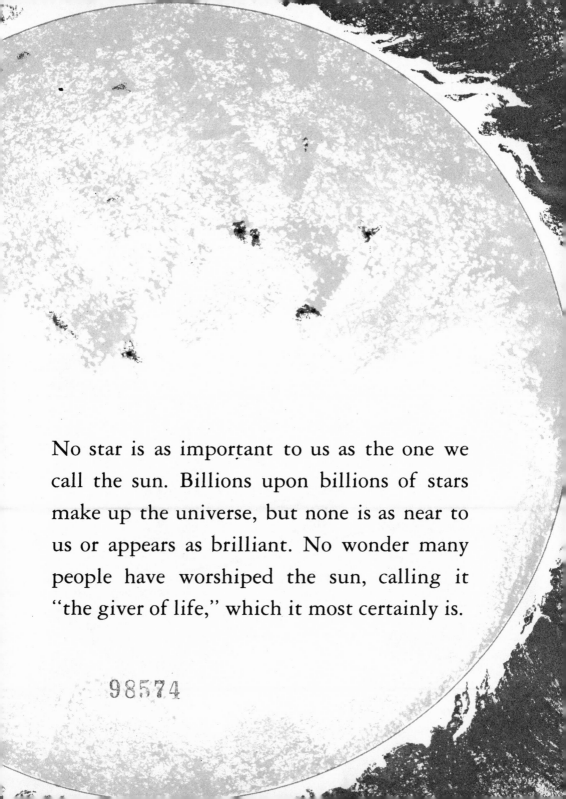

No star is as important to us as the one we
call the sun. Billions upon billions of stars
make up the universe, but none is as near to
us or appears as brilliant. No wonder many
people have worshiped the sun, calling it
"the giver of life," which it most certainly is.

98574

Spaceships have taken astronauts to the moon. Unmanned spacecraft have gone to Mercury, Venus, Mars, and Jupiter. But a spaceship venturing within fifty million kilometers of the sun would become dangerously hot.

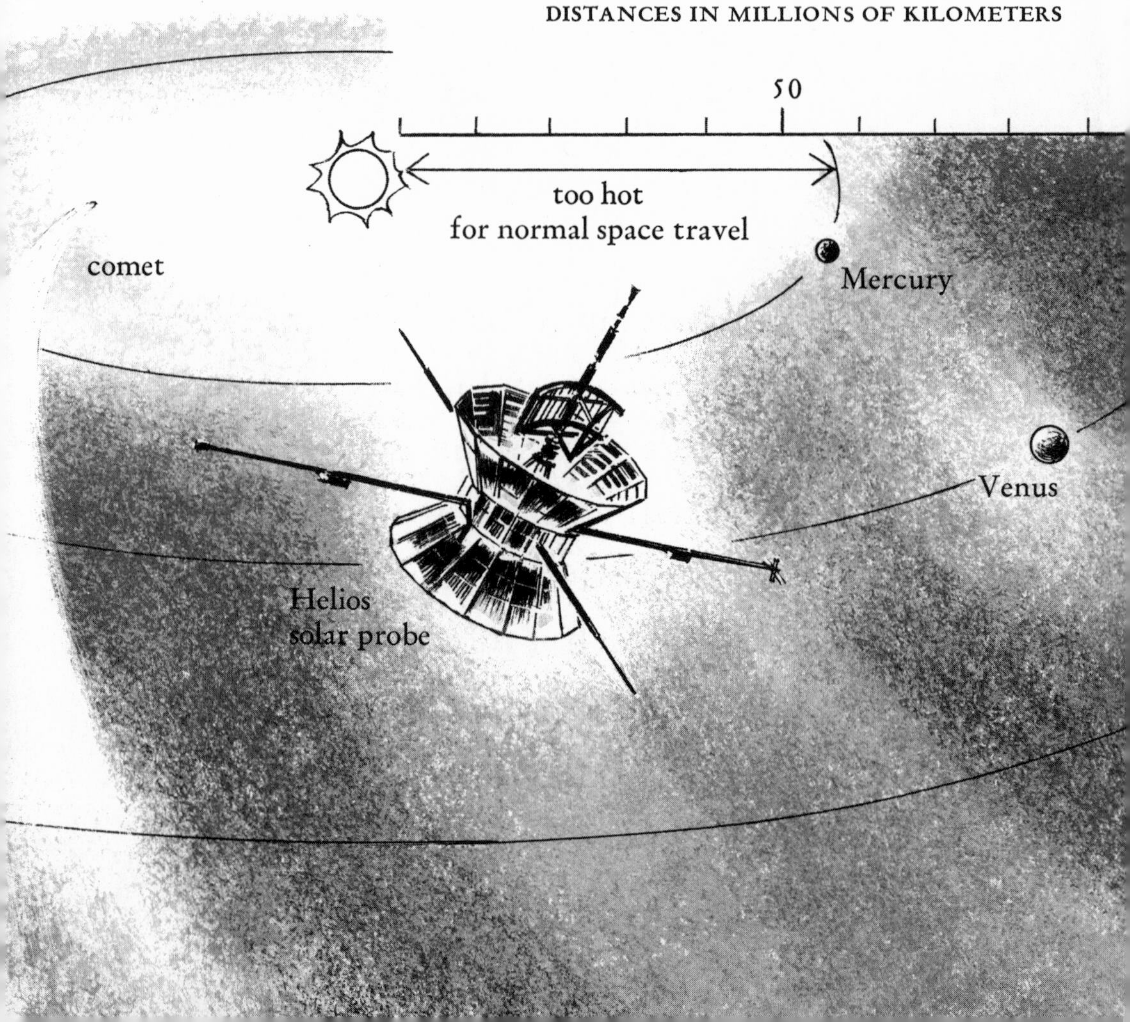

DISTANCES IN MILLIONS OF KILOMETERS

50

too hot
for normal space travel

comet

Mercury

Venus

Helios
solar probe

Even so, we know much about what our sun is like and what is happening there. Electrons, protons, and other atomic particles stream out from the sun. So does energy as light, ultraviolet, and radio waves. These give us clues to the nature of our sun.

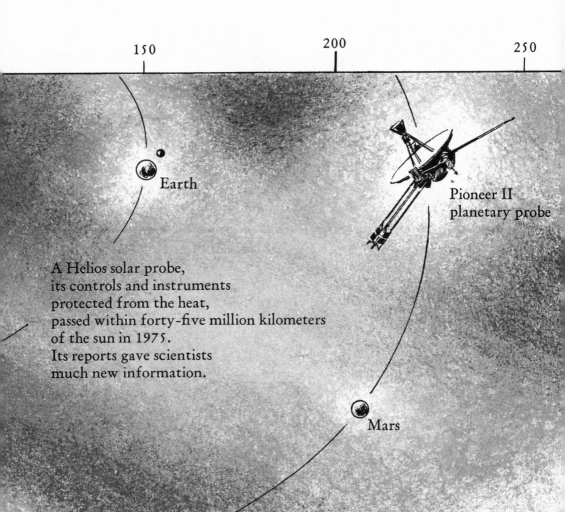

150   200   250

Earth

Pioneer II
planetary probe

A Helios solar probe,
its controls and instruments
protected from the heat,
passed within forty-five million kilometers
of the sun in 1975.
Its reports gave scientists
much new information.

Mars

Long before space travel, people were watching, studying, and arguing about the sun. But the scientific study of our nearest star can be dated from 1770 when its distance was first measured accurately. Within another century we learned the sun's size, its

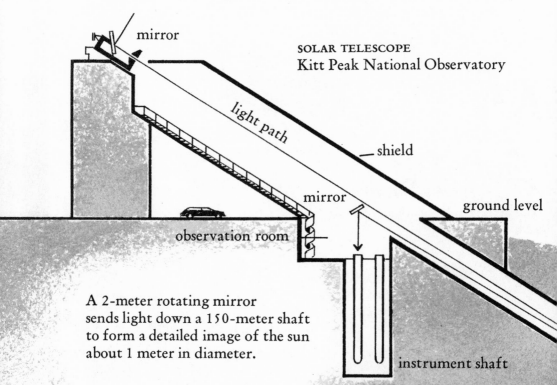

SOLAR TELESCOPE
Kitt Peak National Observatory

mirror

light path

shield

mirror

ground level

observation room

A 2-meter rotating mirror
sends light down a 150-meter shaft
to form a detailed image of the sun
about 1 meter in diameter.

instrument shaft

mass or weight, its brightness and temperature. Later we discovered the secret of its great heat.

The temperature, measured at the surface of the sun, averages about 5800°C. This is some four times higher than that of melting iron. At that temperature rocks and everything else on earth would be a glowing gas.

TEMPERATURES AT WHICH SOME THINGS MELT
(in degrees Celsius)

osmium	2700°C	silver	960°C
molybdenum	2622	salt	804
boron	2300	aluminum	660
chromium	1900	zinc	419
iron	1535	lead	327
uranium	1150	sulfur	215
glass	1050	paraffin	55
gold	963	ice	0

mirror

The temperature inside the sun cannot be measured directly, but it may be as much as 15 million degrees at the center where the pressure is greatest. No ordinary fuel can produce such heat. If the sun were burning coal, its temperature would be much lower and it would have burned out centuries ago.

A ball of coal
the size of the sun
would burn up completely
in about 3000 years,
and would give much less heat.

The sun has been "burning"
for over five billion years,
and it will last
for billions of years more.

wood 60

alcohol 114   coal 122

jet fuel 166

gasoline 166

When the same amounts
of different fuels are burned,
different amounts of heat are produced.
Figures are thousands of calories
per kilogram of fuel.

acetylene 189
hydrogen 544

Odd as it may seem, the temperatures on the sun are too hot to be caused by the kind of burning that we know on earth. When fuels burn, they combine with oxygen from the air. The carbon of wood, coal, or oil joins with oxygen to form molecules of carbon-dioxide gas. But at temperatures of 5800°C. the chemical elements have so much energy that they cannot unite and form molecules as they usually do when burning.

Astronomers believe that the sun has been shrinking, or contracting, which can account for some of its heat. But the sun gives out a thousand times as much heat as contraction alone could produce. The secret of the sun's heat was finally discovered about 1940.

Astronomers are now sure that the sun and other stars are great nuclear furnaces. In them, atoms of hydrogen are changed to helium. The change is not simple. It occurs in two places. The first is deep in the sun, the second closer to the surface.

Shrinking, or contracting, could not have accounted for the sun's heat for as long a time as it has been active.

a shrinking sun

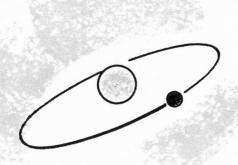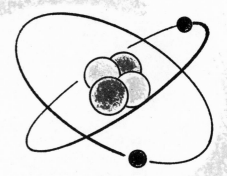

Every second on the sun,
600,000,000,000 kilograms of hydrogen
are changed to helium.
This is the source of the sun's heat.

In the first case, atoms of the elements carbon and nitrogen are formed. These atoms break down, releasing helium. Direct collisions also change hydrogen to helium. The core, or nucleus, of each hydrogen atom is a proton. Four protons may join to form the nucleus of a helium atom, which is four times heavier. This proton-to-proton change is most common and most important on the sun.

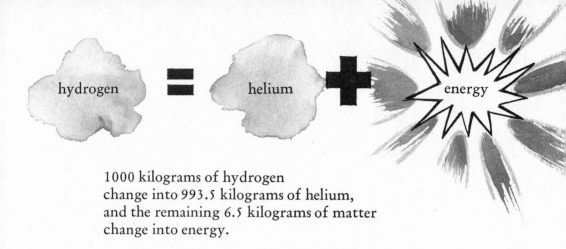

hydrogen = helium + energy

1000 kilograms of hydrogen
change into 993.5 kilograms of helium,
and the remaining 6.5 kilograms of matter
change into energy.

A ton of hydrogen does not become a ton of helium; it ends up weighing about 6.5 kg. less. This small amount of the sun's material becomes radiant energy mainly in the form of light. When matter is thus changed to energy, tremendous amounts of it result. The amount is much, much greater than when fuel is burned in the usual way.

Einstein showed, in his famous equation,
that when matter is changed into energy,
a tremendous amount of energy is formed.
This simple equation is the basis
for the energy of the universe.

$$E = MC^2$$

Albert Einstein and others worked out this change of matter into energy. What happens on the sun is something like a hydrogen bomb exploding. Because the sun is so large even the tiny fraction of its matter that is changed into energy is enormous. It comes to four million tons a second.

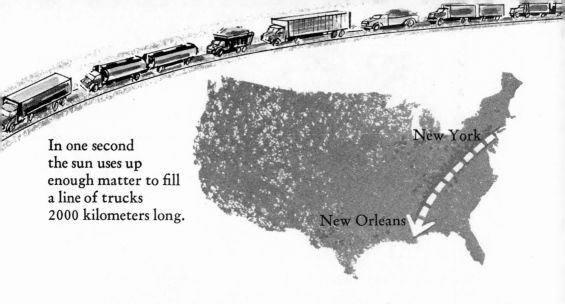

In one second the sun uses up enough matter to fill a line of trucks 2000 kilometers long.

New York

New Orleans

Four million tons a second is next to nothing compared to the total weight of the sun. Yet the matter used in one second could fill a line of trucks almost 2000 km. long — from New York to New Orleans. The sun has been converting matter into energy at this rate for well over five billion years. It can continue for another five billion at least.

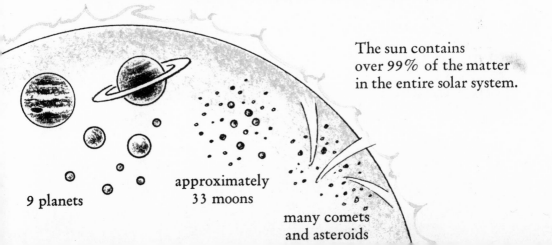

The sun contains over 99% of the matter in the entire solar system.

9 planets

approximately 33 moons

many comets and asteroids

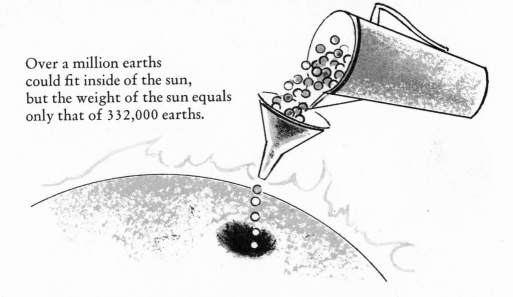

Over a million earths
could fit inside of the sun,
but the weight of the sun equals
only that of 332,000 earths.

Our sun is only an average, middle-sized star. If it were hollow, over a million earths could fit inside. But its density (its weight compared to its volume) is low. So the sun weighs only as much as a third of a million earths.

The density of the earth is 5.5, which is to say that it weighs 5.5 times as much as a ball of water the same size. Mercury, Venus, and Mars have similar densities. But the density of the sun is only 1.4. It is about the same as that of Jupiter and the other large planets.

Until we know more about the past history of the sun, we cannot fully explain the differences in density of the sun, the planets, and our moon.

DENSITIES

Sun 1.4 Jupiter 1.3 Saturn 0.7

Venus 5.1 Earth 5.5 Moon 3.5

The sun is made of gases, not of solid materials like the earth. We think of gases as something like air. A gas heavier than water, which has a density of 1, is hard to imagine, but so is everything about the sun.

The strange, heavy gases on the sun are partly due to the sun's huge weight, which gives it a pull, or gravity, about 30 times that of the earth. This force and the high temperatures create conditions that are almost impossible to duplicate on our planet. Still, we have made conditions like those on the sun on a small scale for a very, very short time.

Scientists are learning how to use the sun's kind of energy to work for us in controlled atomic fusion. Fusion atomic energy is already in use, but it still has many unresolved problems.

Scientists will never learn firsthand what the inside of the sun is like. There the gases are even denser. Temperature and pressure are so high that electrons and protons are stripped from atoms, causing changes that have not been seen here on earth.

The sun's surface, or photosphere, seen through special telescopes, is covered with grainy spots, or granules, some 300 to 1000 km. in diameter. The surface is not like the earth's, but more like the outer face of a thick glowing cloud. The granules may be spurts of rising, hot gases. Their darker rims may be sinking cooler gases.

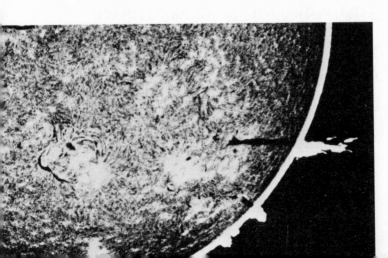

The surface, or photosphere, of the sun photographed with hydrogen light.

High Altitude Observatory, National Center for Atmospheric Research

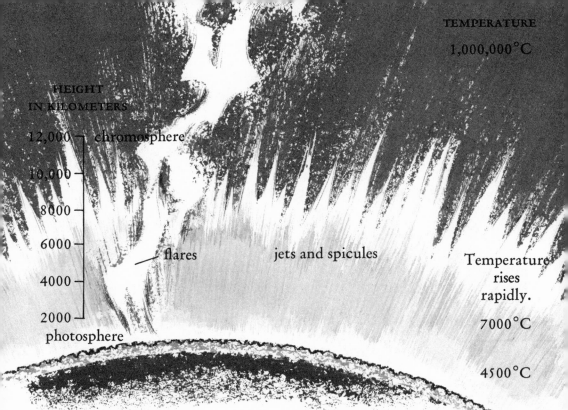

TEMPERATURE

1,000,000°C

HEIGHT
IN KILOMETERS

12,000 — chromosphere

10,000 —

8000 —

6000 —

flares   jets and spicules   Temperature
                                            rises
4000 —   rapidly.

                                            7000°C
2000 —
photosphere   4500°C

Above the surface lies the atmosphere of the
sun. Its inner part, the chromosphere, has two
layers. The lower one, relatively cool, is about
4000 km. thick. Above it, in a layer about
8000 km. thick, the gases thin out rapidly,
but their temperature rises to perhaps one
million degrees C.

Jets and streams of glowing gases rise through the chromosphere. Some are so large they dwarf the earth. Most may come from the granules in the photosphere. Thousands of these jets and streamers of gas form and disappear every moment. They may speed the movement of radiant energy out of the sun. Flares appear before sunspots. Prominences rise, twist, and spiral out as far as 900,000 km.

Large prominence on the sun, over 200,000 kilometers high
Hale Observatories

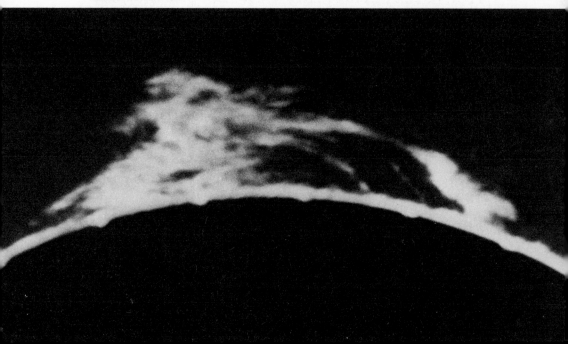

Corona of the sun
with many streamers,
taken during an eclipse.
High Altitude Observatory,
National Center
for Atmospheric Research

The famous corona of the sun is the last visible part of its atmosphere. It may be the source of much of the sun's ultraviolet light. The faint glow of the corona's very thin gases extends out millions of km. This soft light can be seen only when light from the sun's disc is cut off, as during an eclipse of the sun. Now it can be photographed at any time with a special instrument.

The excited atoms in the corona, changed by the very high temperature, give out a very special kind of light. Sunspots and magnetic storms on the sun alter the corona too.

Radiant energy from the sun pours out in all directions like warmth from a campfire. Light is visible radiant energy. Other waves of radiation, like heat, ultraviolet, X rays, and radio, are invisible.

Ultraviolet light is of special interest. It causes tanning and sunburn when you are at the beach. It kills germs and makes a fluorescent tube glow. Luckily, most ultraviolet light we get from the sun is blocked by the upper layers of our atmosphere. If all of it reached the ground, it would be dangerous to human beings and most every other kind of life.

Light waves of different lengths make up visible sunlight. When sunlight is passed through a spectroscope, the glass prism in this instrument bends the rays of light. Short waves bend most, longer ones less. Thus, what appeared as white light is spread out into a ribbon of different wavelengths. They make a pattern of colors, from red and orange to green, blue, and violet, called the solar spectrum.

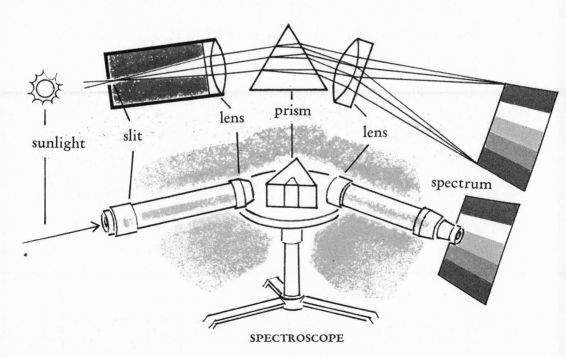

SPECTROSCOPE

red yellow green violet

A rainbow is a natural solar spectrum
formed when sunlight is broken up
by raindrops instead of by a glass prism.

The colorful band of the solar spectrum is crossed by many dark lines. They mark places where light from the sun's photosphere is blocked or absorbed by gases in its chromosphere. In the laboratory these dark lines are compared with bright spectrum lines produced when a chemical element is heated till it glows. When the lines match, they identify the chemical element on the sun. By this method about 70 of the 92 natural elements have been found on the sun.

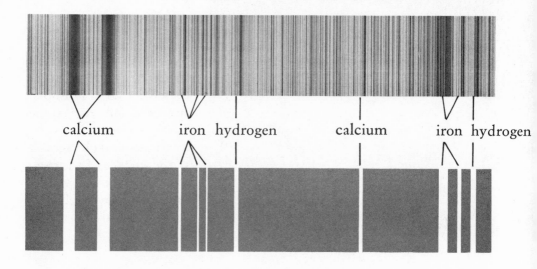

SOLAR SPECTRUM
The lines in the spectrum of the sun or other star
tell what chemical elements are present.
They also give clues to temperature, pressure,
and other physical conditions.
Magnetic and electrical fields have been discovered
by studying spectra and from them
the movement and speed of stars can be estimated.

The first time the solar spectroscope was
used, new lines were seen that did not match
those of any known element. The new element, thus discovered, was named helium
for the sun. It was later found here on earth.

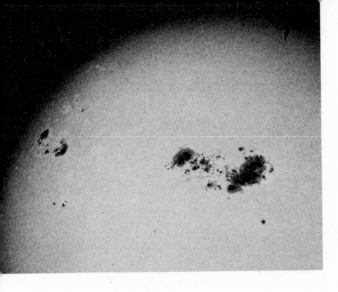

In 1947,
these very large sunspots
appeared and were studied.
They help us
to understand changes
at the surface of the sun
and the ways
that these may affect
our planet earth.

Hale Observatories

Sunspots are closely related to flares and their bright areas. They start as many small specks that come together to make larger sunspots. These dark spots and blotches are easily seen. They look dark, because they are a bit cooler than other areas of the photosphere. But their temperature of about 4500°C. is hotter than any earthly flame. Even small sunspots are larger than the earth. A few large ones have measured 150,000 km. across and more.

This detail
of a large sunspot
shows why astronomers
once believed
that sunspots were holes
through which one could
look deep into the sun.
Compare this
with the size
of the earth, below.
Princeton University Observatory

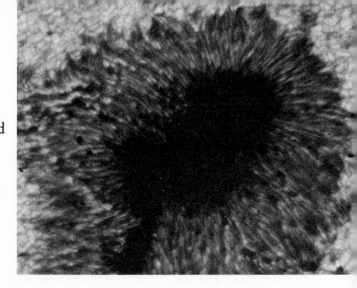

Sunspots move, grow, and finally disappear. Much of their motion is due to the motion of the sun. At its equator the sun rotates in 25 days. Near its poles it rotates more slowly. A sunspot that appears at the center of the sun's disc will move steadily toward the edge in 6 days or so.

The regular movement of sunspots
proves that the sun is rotating.

second day   seventh day   twelfth day

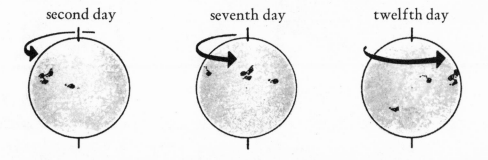

As it grows big, a less dark area forms around the sunspot. Often sunspots appear in pairs or in groups. They may last a day or a week, but a few remain for an entire month or more.

Over a century ago it was discovered
that sunspots come in cycles.
Their number increases year after year for five or six years
and then begins to fall off to a low point again.
Each cycle lasts about ten years,
but why there are cycles at all, we do not know.

AVERAGE NUMBER
OF SUNSPOTS

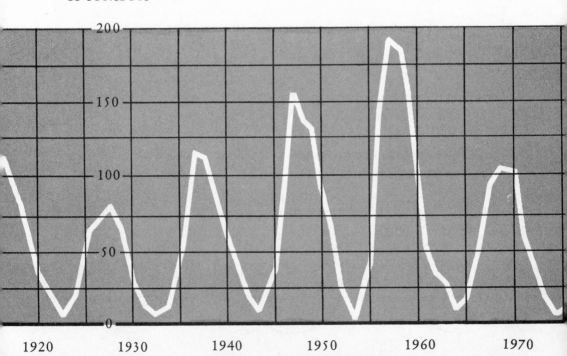

About every eleven years, on the average, sunspots reach their maximum number. Then a dozen or more and sometimes as many as a hundred may be seen at one time. Five or six years later few, if any, sunspots are seen. Gradually they become more and more common, till they reach their peak again. This sunspot cycle has been as short as eight and as long as sixteen years.

At the start of the cycle, sunspots begin to form about a third of the distance from the sun's equator to its poles. As time passes, they form closer and closer to the equator, but they never quite reach it. The regions from the poles halfway to the equator rarely have any sunspots at all.

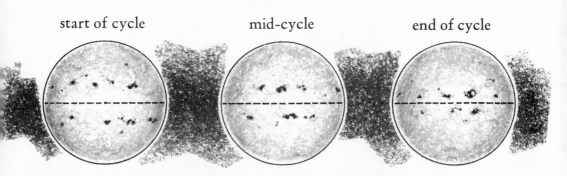

start of cycle   mid-cycle   end of cycle

The earth behaves like a huge magnet. So does the sun, but its magnetism reverses every 22 years. In addition, sunspots act like small but very powerful magnets — each a hundred or even several thousand times as strong as the earth's magnetism.

Solar flares and sunspots send electrons and protons out at speeds of about 1500 km. a second. The sun is some 150 million km. from the earth, so in about a day these charged particles reach us. The ultraviolet light from the sun travels 300,000 km. per second. It reaches us in only 8.3 minutes.

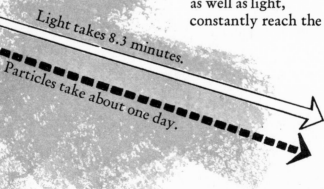

sun

Light takes 8.3 minutes.

Particles take about one day.

Charged particles from the sun, as well as light, constantly reach the earth.

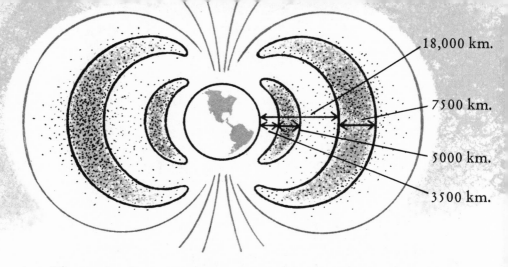

18,000 km.

7500 km.

5000 km.

3500 km.

The earth's magnetic field and particles trapped in it

The charged particles from the sun first affect the earth's curved magnetic belts that extend far out from our two poles. Then they blanket the sunny side of the earth, causing electrical disturbances. Television, radio, and long-distance telephone signals fade or become garbled when sunspots are numerous. The compass needle may wander on small ships and planes. This could be a serious source of trouble.

In ways not very well understood, sunspots may also affect the earth and life upon it. Astronomers are curious when they learn that similar eleven-year cycles have been recognized in the growth and behavior of plants and animals. If sunspots really are the cause, how they act is yet to be discovered.

For example, when sunspots are increasing rapidly, the earth's temperature seems to drop about 3°C. below normal. As the sunspot cycle moves toward its low point, the populations of wild rabbits and the foxes that feed on them seem to rise. The growth of trees may be faster when sunspots are increasing. Reports say that trees grow taller as the sunspot cycle reaches its peak, and they become thicker too, as shown in the growth rings.

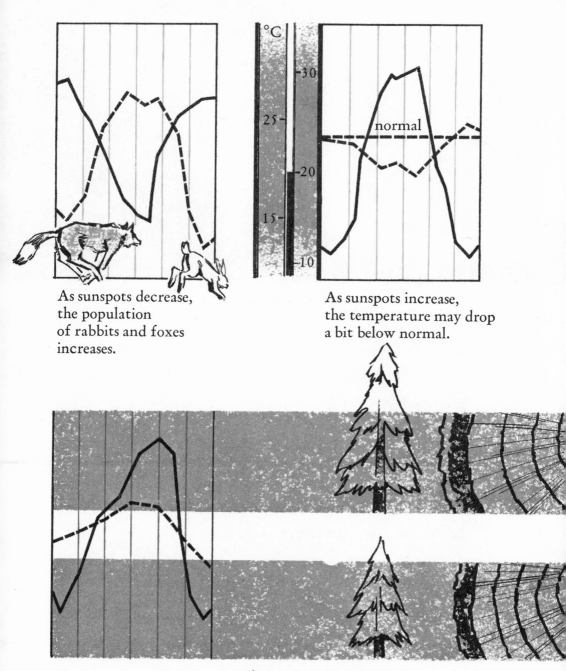

As sunspots decrease,
the population
of rabbits and foxes
increases.

As sunspots increase,
the temperature may drop
a bit below normal.

As sunspots increase,
trees may grow taller,
with thicker trunks.

Particles from the sun produce the aurora borealis.
Robert A. Bumpas, National Center for Atmospheric Research

In areas far north and south of the equator
and a hundred or more miles up, the same
charged particles from the sun cause the thin
gases of the air to glow. The flickering, shift-
ing colors that form are called the aurora
borealis, or northern lights.

Saturn
80 minutes

Jupiter
42 minutes

It is hard to realize the great amount of radiant energy that pours from the sun, year after year and century after century. Only one two-billionth of it reaches the earth. Practically all the light and heat from the sun goes out into the empty vastness of space.

All radiant energy travels at the same speed — 300,000 km. a second. In three minutes light from the sun reaches Mercury. In six minutes it passes Venus. In a bit over eight minutes it reaches our earth.

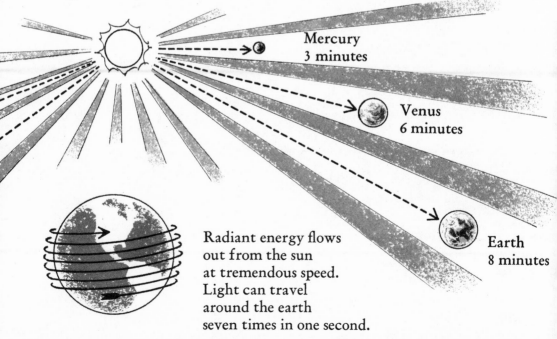

Mercury
3 minutes

Venus
6 minutes

Earth
8 minutes

Radiant energy flows
out from the sun
at tremendous speed.
Light can travel
around the earth
seven times in one second.

Clouds reflect some of this sunlight back into space. Some is scattered and absorbed by the air, making the sky seem blue. A total of about 35 percent is lost; the rest is absorbed or reflected by the seas and the land. It is transmitted in many ways, through living and nonliving things. Sooner or later this radiant energy, changed into longer waves, is radiated back into the atmosphere and is finally lost in space.

WHAT HAPPENS TO SUNLIGHT

About 42% is reflected back into space.

About 15% is absorbed and scattered.

About 43% reaches the ground. It is absorbed but is later radiated out as heat.

The value of the solar energy the earth receives cannot be reckoned in dollars. At the cheapest rate, the amount of electricity needed to equal the energy the earth gets free from the sun would cost many thousands of billions of dollars a day. At this rate, New York City alone gets over half a billion dollars' worth of sunlight daily.

The energy we get from the sun, if totally used, would do work at a rate equal to about 30,000 horsepower for every person on earth.

A small electric motor rates 1 horsepower or less.

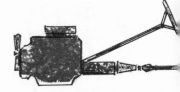

An automobile rates at about 150 horsepower.

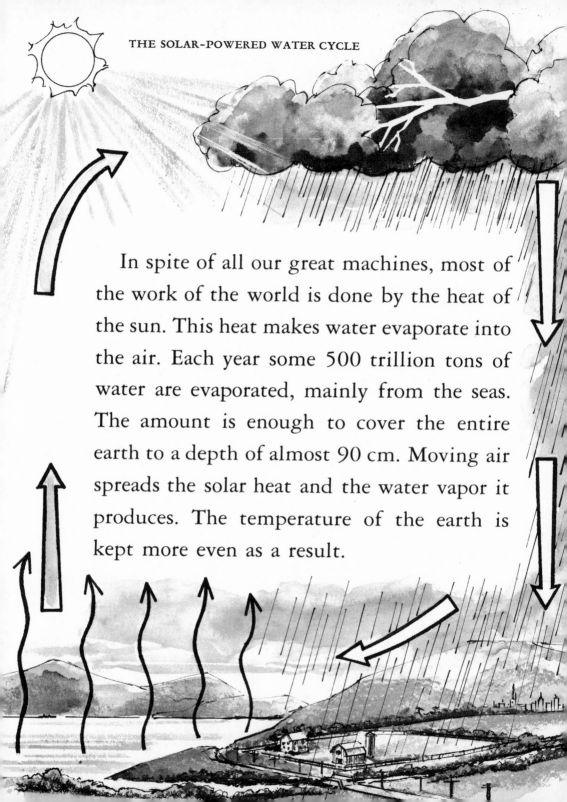

In spite of all our great machines, most of the work of the world is done by the heat of the sun. This heat makes water evaporate into the air. Each year some 500 trillion tons of water are evaporated, mainly from the seas. The amount is enough to cover the entire earth to a depth of almost 90 cm. Moving air spreads the solar heat and the water vapor it produces. The temperature of the earth is kept more even as a result.

Warm air holds up to four percent moisture. When it cools, it can hold less, and some falls as rain or snow. The amount each year about equals the water that evaporates. Rain that falls on the land makes plants grow. It keeps animals alive. It flows into brooks, rivers, and lakes. Solar energy makes fresh water from seawater and carries it far inland.

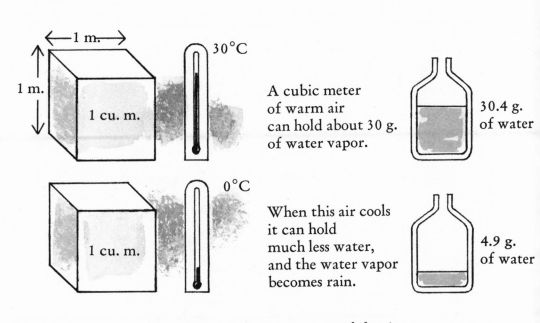

A cubic meter of warm air can hold about 30 g. of water vapor.

30.4 g. of water

When this air cools it can hold much less water, and the water vapor becomes rain.

4.9 g. of water

Solar heat and the movements of the air take water from the salty sea and drop it as fresh rain in many distant places.

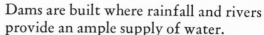
Dams are built where rainfall and rivers provide an ample supply of water.

We dam rivers and store water to prevent floods. We take some to irrigate the land, so crops will grow better. The water behind the dam is used for people's enjoyment. The water over the dam turns dynamos and makes some of our electricity. All this is possible, because the sun's heat has made water evaporate.

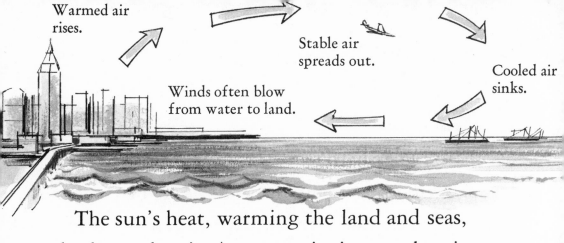

Warmed air rises.

Stable air spreads out.

Cooled air sinks.

Winds often blow from water to land.

The sun's heat, warming the land and seas, also heats the air. As warm air rises, cooler air moves in over the ground and patterns of winds are set up. Solar heat also causes the currents in the oceans, such as the famous Gulf Stream. The different climates all over the world come from the flow of solar heat over land and sea.

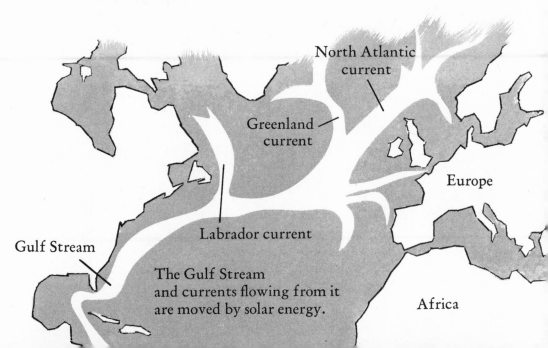

North Atlantic current

Greenland current

Europe

Labrador current

Gulf Stream

The Gulf Stream and currents flowing from it are moved by solar energy.

Africa

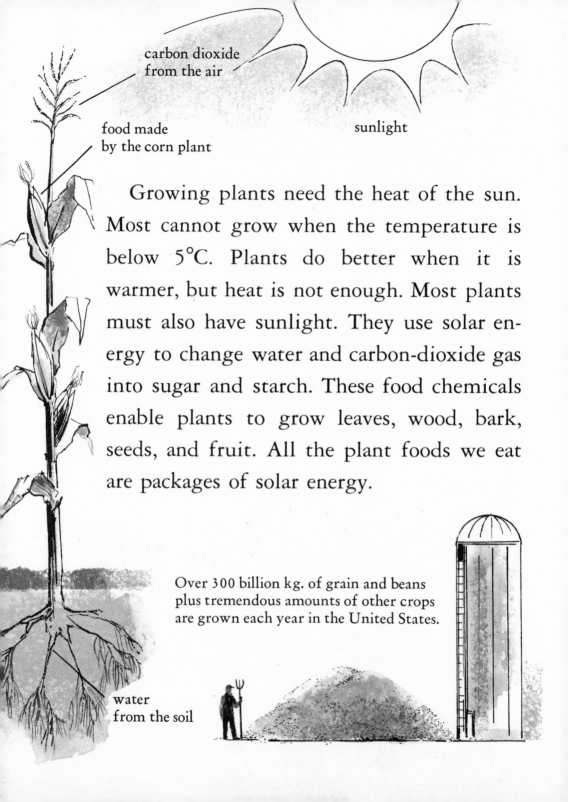

carbon dioxide
from the air

food made
by the corn plant

sunlight

Growing plants need the heat of the sun. Most cannot grow when the temperature is below 5°C. Plants do better when it is warmer, but heat is not enough. Most plants must also have sunlight. They use solar energy to change water and carbon-dioxide gas into sugar and starch. These food chemicals enable plants to grow leaves, wood, bark, seeds, and fruit. All the plant foods we eat are packages of solar energy.

Over 300 billion kg. of grain and beans plus tremendous amounts of other crops are grown each year in the United States.

water
from the soil

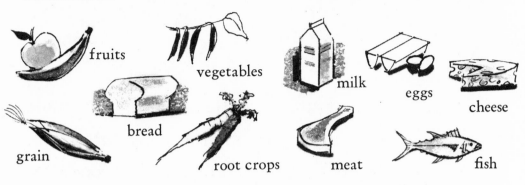

fruits

vegetables

milk

eggs

cheese

bread

grain

root crops

meat

fish

Plants have been growing and making food for hundreds of millions of years. Long ago storms and floods buried plants in the mud of rivers and swamps. These layers of plant material slowly changed to the peat and coal we now burn to heat our buildings and run our factories. Coal is sometimes called "buried sunlight" — and it is exactly that.

Buried plants become peat and coal.

Tiny plants
that make
petroleum
(enlarged)

In ancient times small sea plants also made food with the aid of sunlight, day after day for millions of years. The surplus food was stored as oils, which slowly changed into dark, thick petroleum. Each year about 3.3 billion barrels of petroleum are pumped from United States wells. From it we make gasoline, motor oil, and hundreds of other chemicals. Automobiles run on sunlight also.

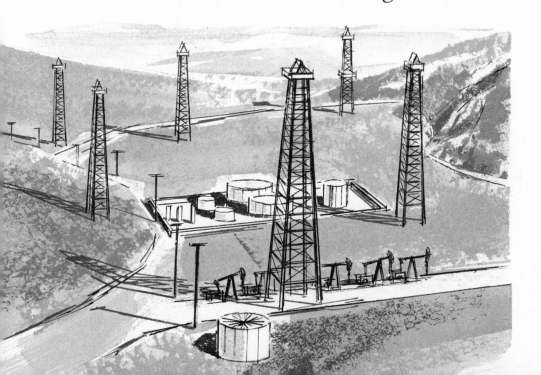

Men have worked for years to make engines to use the heat of the sun directly. Some have curved mirrors to focus, or bring together, the sun's rays at one very hot spot. Solar heat can boil water and change it into steam. Small solar stoves cook food or bake bread. But these devices work well only in the hotter, drier parts of the world. Someday pumps run by solar engines may bring enough water to the deserts so crops can grow there.

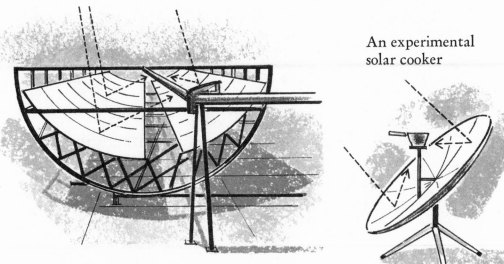

An experimental
solar cooker

A solar engine
that ran a steam-driven pump

In winter, the sun is low.
Sunlight enters and warms the house.

Even where solar engines cannot be used, solar heat can work to heat homes. A solar house is built with large windows facing south. In winter, when the sun is low, the house is warmed by sunlight. When the sun is higher in the summer sky, an overhanging roof keeps the sunlight out. At night and on cloudy days, other kinds of heat may be needed. A solar heater on the roof can also provide hot water.

solar water heater

In summer, the sun is high. An overhang keeps the sunlight out.

In modern solar houses heat collected on the roof is absorbed and stored in tanks of chemicals. It is released and used at night. Newer models change some of the solar heat directly into electricity for immediate use or storage in batteries. Solar heat can also be stored in chemical salts. In this kind of complete solar house, the sun's heat can even run air conditioners for cooling. Such houses are still being tested.

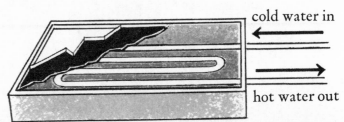

A solar heater on the roof can supply hot water.

cold water in

hot water out

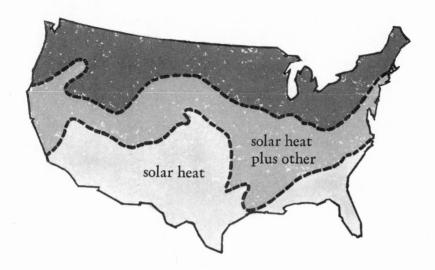

Solar heat

solar heat
plus other

Solar heating works well only
where the climate is favorable.
In warm places enough solar heat is available
to heat (or cool) the entire house.
In other areas solar heat can help save fuel.
Below is an experimental solar house
at the University of Delaware.

Institute of Energy Conversion, University of Delaware

Nearly every bit of light we see can be traced back to the sun. You read this book only because light is reflected from the page back to your eyes. When about 400 trillion light waves a second are reflected, a cloth looks red. About 600 trillion make the color green, and about 800 trillion put violet before your eyes.

The binding of this book looks yellow, because it absorbs the red, orange, green, and blue waves that are part of sunlight. Only the yellow rays are reflected. Red rays are reflected from a ripe apple, and green rays from grass. Absorption, reflection, and bending of light waves make things look as they do.

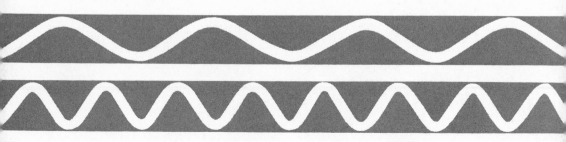

Long waves of red light and shorter waves of violet

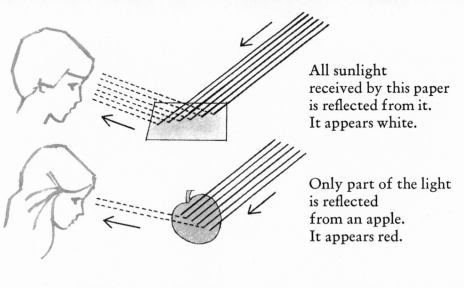

All sunlight
received by this paper
is reflected from it.
It appears white.

Only part of the light
is reflected
from an apple.
It appears red.

When sunlight passes through raindrops in just the right way, each drop acts like a tiny glass prism. The light is bent and spread out, so the color bands separate into a rainbow. You see this naturally curved spectrum best when the sun is behind you. Sometimes a double rainbow forms with reversed colors.

A rainbow breaks sunlight up
and separates the different
wavelengths of light.

sunlight

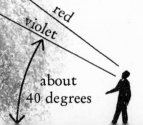

red

violet

about
40 degrees

All sunlight comes through the layer of air around the earth. At sunrise and sunset, the sunlight passes through a thicker air layer than at noon when the sun is highest. The thicker layer of air absorbs more blue and violet rays, so the sun appears much redder than it does in the middle of the day. Red and orange rays are not absorbed as much as blue and violet.

noon

At noon the sun is highest in the sky,
and in some places it is overhead or nearly so.
Then the rays pass through only a thin layer of air.
At sunrise and sunset, because of the lower angle,
the sun's light passes through a much thicker layer of air.
The violet and blue rays are absorbed or scattered.
The sunlight becomes more orange and red,
and tints the clouds and sky with these colors.

sunrise

sunset

The earth and the other planets were formed from the sun over five billion years ago. But only a bit of solar material was used. At least 99 percent remains in the sun, which is much larger and heavier than all the planets together. As a result, the sun's pull, or gravity, is so great that it easily holds all the planets in their paths, or orbits. These orbits are almost as round as circles. Were this pull of the sun any different, the planets would have different orbits, or they might even shoot straight out into space.

As a result of these two pulls, the earth travels in an orbit around the sun.

The sun, because of its great mass, is constantly pulling the earth toward it.

Otherwise, because of its speed, the earth would shoot off into space in a straight line.

The pull of the sun and moon makes the tides in our ocean. Twice a day, in most places, the level of the water rises and falls. Because the moon, though smaller, is much nearer, its pull is stronger. When the sun and moon pull in the same line, as they do twice a month, tides are highest. In a few places, because of the shape of the Pacific basin, the pull of the moon has no effect. Instead, the tides follow the sun, and on some small mid-Pacific islands high tide always comes at noon.

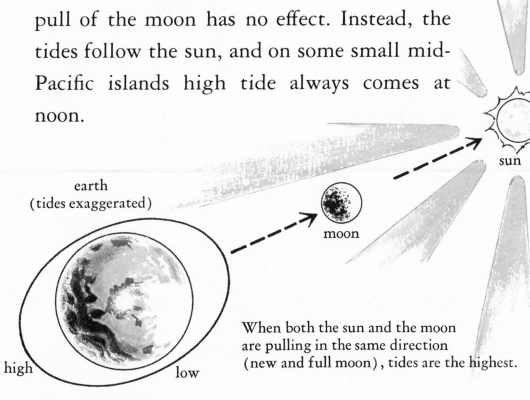

earth
(tides exaggerated)

moon

sun

high

low

When both the sun and the moon are pulling in the same direction (new and full moon), tides are the highest.

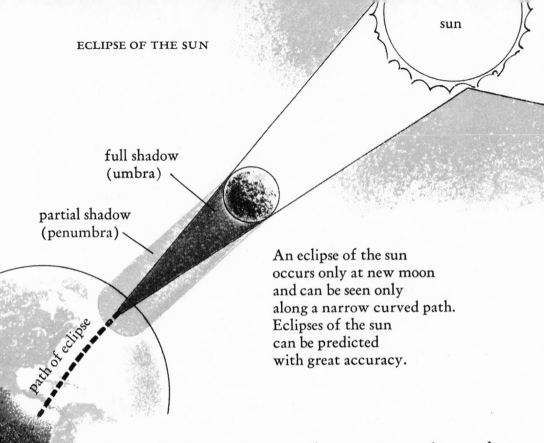

sun

full shadow
(umbra)

partial shadow
(penumbra)

path of eclipse

An eclipse of the sun
occurs only at new moon
and can be seen only
along a narrow curved path.
Eclipses of the sun
can be predicted
with great accuracy.

Several times a year the sun, earth, and moon are exactly in line for a short time. As the moon comes between the sun and the earth, two to five times a year, we may see an eclipse of the sun. This event is a rare and exciting sight as the moon's shadow slowly blacks out the disc of the sun.

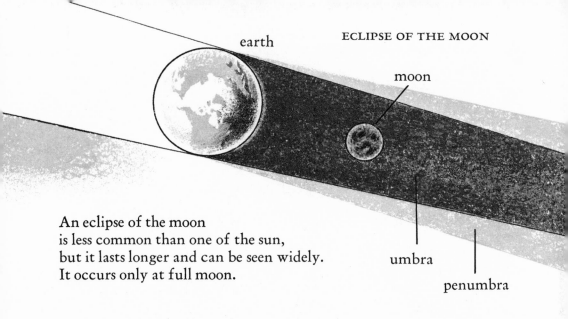

earth

moon

An eclipse of the moon
is less common than one of the sun,
but it lasts longer and can be seen widely.
It occurs only at full moon.

umbra

penumbra

An eclipse of the moon occurs up to three times a year when the earth comes between the moon and the sun. It is not exciting, but it is well worth seeing. The earth's shadow is larger than the moon, so an eclipse of the moon lasts longer than a solar eclipse.

Because the sun, moon, and earth move exactly on schedule, astronomers can figure out, years in advance, when an eclipse will occur. They can predict it to the exact minute.

For a true picture of the sun, we must compare it with the thousands upon thousands of other stars that have been studied. The next closest star is some 300,000 times farther away from us than the sun. Many are millions of times farther away. If the sun were as far away as the stars in the Big Dipper, it would be much too faint to be seen.

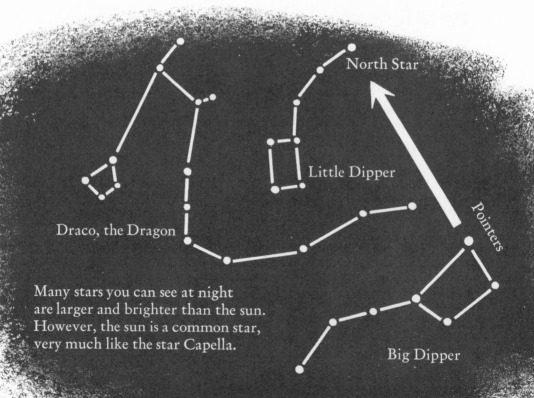

North Star

Little Dipper

Pointers

Draco, the Dragon

Many stars you can see at night are larger and brighter than the sun. However, the sun is a common star, very much like the star Capella.

Big Dipper

red	yellow	blue-white
Cool stars show neutral metals and chemical molecules. Antares is an example.	Medium stars show some metals, especially calcium. The sun and Capella are two examples.	Hot stars have charged elements and some neutral helium. Riga and Spica are examples.

The size, distance, mass, and brightness of stars have been measured. Their color tells their temperature. Cool red stars are about 2600°C., yellow stars, of which our sun is an example, measure 6000°C., and bright blue-white stars may reach 21,000°C. or more.

The hottest stars are about six times as hot as our sun. The coolest ones are half as hot. But when studying a small group of stars that are nearest to the sun, astronomers found that the sun is fourth brightest in that group.

To the left is a part
of the largest star,
and 400 suns could fit
across its center,
side by side.
To the right is the sun,
and 200 white dwarf
stars could fit
across its center,
side by side.
The sun is
average size.

In size, the sun also runs a bit below the average. It takes four hundred suns, side by side, to fit across the center of the largest star. But only about two hundred of the smallest white dwarf stars would fit across our sun. If compared in size to neutron stars, however, our sun may well be a giant.

The sun is very much like other stars. About 90 percent of it is hydrogen, and this gas is also very common on other stars as well. About 10 percent of the sun is helium, which is common on other stars too. All other chemical elements found on the sun are present in small amounts. Other stars, especially the oldest ones, may have less of these other elements.

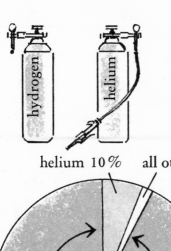

The sun is like many medium-hot stars. But stars do change with age and, as they become cooler, the chemicals in them form new combinations. These are the most common elements in our sun.

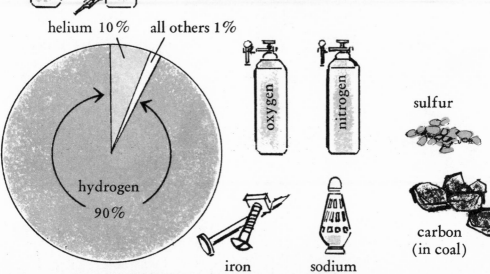

helium 10%   all others 1%

hydrogen 90%

oxygen

nitrogen

sulfur

iron

sodium (in salt)

carbon (in coal)

While the sun turns on its axis, it is also moving through space in the general direction of the star Vega at a speed of about 20 km. a second. All the planets move along with it.

The sun is moving on its own, but it also is moving, or revolving, as part of a much larger family of stars. This star family is our galaxy, a great group of about 200 billion stars spread out over distances that are hard to imagine. Our galaxy has the shape of a wheel with a bulging center, from which several spiral arms extend. The sun, in one of these arms, revolves around the center of the galaxy in about 200 million years. When you see the Milky Way at night, you are looking toward these spiral arms and the home of our small sun.

A nearby galaxy, quite like our own,
in the constellation Andromeda.

Hale Observatories

So our sun, like a grain of sand on the beach, is only one of billions of stars. Yet it is a common kind. About one fifth of all the stars studied are of the same general type. It is medium sized, medium hot, medium heavy, and not especially outstanding. But it is familiar to us all. For us, it is the most important star in the whole universe.

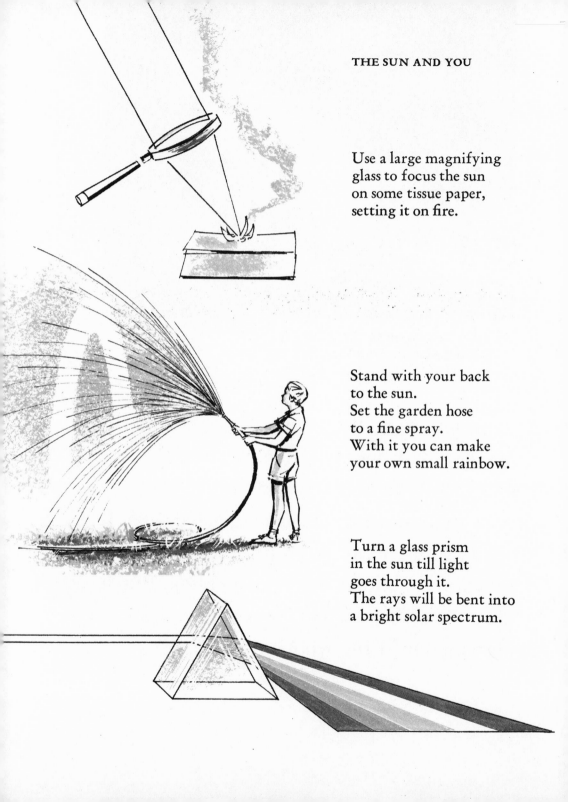

Use a large magnifying
glass to focus the sun
on some tissue paper,
setting it on fire.

Stand with your back
to the sun.
Set the garden hose
to a fine spray.
With it you can make
your own small rainbow.

Turn a glass prism
in the sun till light
goes through it.
The rays will be bent into
a bright solar spectrum.

Plant five beans
in each of two flowerpots.
Water both but cover one
with a heavy bag
to keep out the sun.
Take a quick look
every day for two weeks
and see how they grow.

In winter,
soon after a snow, put
a square of black cloth
and the same size square
of aluminum foil
on the snow.
Let the sun shine
on both for an hour,
and see which has
absorbed the most heat
and sunk the deepest.

Hold a pair of binoculars
as shown so the sun shines
through one of the lenses.
See if you can get
an image of the sun
on a sheet of paper.

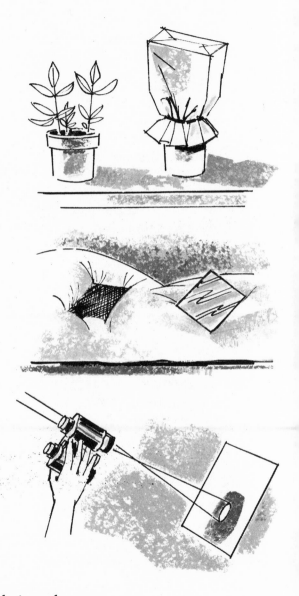

Warning: Looking directly into the sun
for more than a quick glance can injure your eyes
Never look at the sun directly
through binoculars or a telescope.

INDEX

* indicates illustration, chart, or diagram

atmosphere of sun, 19*, 20*-21
atomic particles, 5, 30*
aurora borealis, 34*
chromosphere, 19*-20
composition of sun, 17-18, 24,
    25*, 59*
corona, 21*-22
density of sun, 15*-16*
distance from earth, 30
earth: magnetic field, 31*;
    orbit, 52*
eclipse of moon, 55*
eclipse of sun, 54*
Einstein, Albert, 12, 13*
gravity of moon, 53*
gravity of sun, 17, 52*-53
Helios solar probe, 4*
light waves, 49*-51*, 50*
melting points, 7*
metric measure, 2
Milky Way Galaxy, 60
northern lights. *See* aurora
    borealis
photosphere, 18*, 19*
Pioneer II planetary probe, 5*
planets: densities, 15*-16*;
    distances from sun, 4*-5*
radiant energy, 12*-14*, 22,

34*-35*, 36*
    heat, 5, 10-11*, 22, 35, 40-
    41
    light, 5, 12, 22, 23, 30*,
        34*-35*, 36*, 49*-51*,
        50*
    radio, 5, 22
    ultraviolet, 5, 22, 30*
    X rays, 22
    See also solar energy
size of sun, 15, 58*
solar energy, 37*-48, 38*, 39*,
    40*, 41*, 42*, 43*, 44*,
    45*. *See also* radiant
    energy
solar flares, 20, 26, 30
solar houses, 46*-48*, 47*
solar spectroscope, 23*, 25
solar spectrum, 23*, 24*, 25*
solar telescope, 6*
stars, 56*-57*, 60
sunlight. *See* light waves,
    radiant energy, solar
    energy
sunspots, 20, 26*-29*, 27*,
    28*, 30, 32-33*
surface of sun. *See* photosphere
temperature of sun, 7-9, 8*

98574

DATE DUE

DE 2 1 '76	MAR 3 1 1991	
MAR 31 '77		
MAY 19 '77	OCT. 2 5 1990	
AUG 04 '77	AUG 0 4 1998	
DEC 3 '77	NOV 03 1998	
MAY 10 '79	7 18 '04	
MAY 18 '79		
DEC 10 '79		
MAR 20 '8		
FEB 23 1990		
APR 28 1990		
DEC 07 1992		

J
523.7
Z
Zim, Herbert Spencer
The sun.

Ohio Dominican College Library
1216 Sunbury Road
Columbus, Ohio 43219

DEMCO